ANCHOR BOOKS

ACROSS THE TABLE

First published in Great Britain in 1995 by
ANCHOR BOOKS
1-2 Wainman Road, Woodston,
Peterborough, PE2 7BU

HB ISBN 1 85930 281 5
SB ISBN 1 85930 286 6

Foreword

Anchor Books is a small press, established in 1992, with the aim of promoting readable poetry to as wide an audience as possible.

We hope to establish an outlet for writers of poetry who may have struggled to see their work in print.

The poems presented here have been selected from many entries. Editing proved to be a difficult and daunting task and as the Editor, the final selection was mine.

The poems chosen represent a cross-section of styles and content. They have been sent from all over the world, written by young and old alike, united in the passion for writing poetry.

I trust this selection will delight and please the authors and all those who enjoy reading poetry.

Glenn Jones
Editor

CONTENTS

My Husband	S Barker	1
Trying To Slim	Val Roberts	2
My Mystery Man	Rahmanara Chowdhury	3
Answer To Your Question	Alice Stapleton	4
Day Dusk And Dawn	Marion Bramley	5
Moods	Hilda Whyman	6
Healthy Diet	Gill Cannon	7
The First Snow	Madeline Derrham	8
Going For A Walk	Rosalie Upton	9
Reflections	Eileen Neal	10
Franceschia	M Babbington	11
Music Everywhere	Elsie Gadsby	12
The Old House	Gwendolyn Cameron	13
On Reflection	Barbara Gundry-White	15
Forever	Anne Chaloner	16
Summer's Song	Jean Graham	17
The Signs	Janet Wainwright	18
Wishes And Dreams	Barbara Gearing	19
A Holiday To Remember	Annelyn Jax	20
The Love Within	Philip May	21
Who'd Be A Mother At Christmas Time?	Loraine Jane Banner	22
The Song	A B Hughes	23
The Magician	Linda Blakey	24
Changing Seasons	Elsie Anderson	25
Dickie Dandelion	D A Watson	26
My Four Footed Friend	Mary Fry	27
Me	Charles Hunter	28
Seaside Out Of Season	Joy Pickering	29
Life's Stage	S V Smy	30
Stranger In The Night	Frank McCabe	31
My Love Is Like A Red Red Doze	Catherine Nair	32
Reason To Live (For Mia)	D McKeown	33
Sunday Tea	Sheila Leheup	34
Ode To Dusty	Jane S Simpson	35

Springing In The Rain	Sarah Maycock	36
May To December	Phyllis Harvey	37
Vanquished Dreams	Jean Little	38
Fireside Eyelids	Michael Coey	39
Reflections From A Silver Kettle	A C J Williams	40
En Hiver	Peter Read	41
The Teardrop	Dorothy N Davies	42
I Hear You Crying	Mike Vukasinovic	43
Always	Jane McGarry	`44
Death Of A Troubled Soul	Samantha Ambrose	45
Love	Alexander	46
Seasons Come And Go	David A Howard	48
Pastures New	E K Bainbridge	49
Night At The Fair	A Jones	50
Teddy's Dilemma	K Pendlebury	51
Holly	Amelia Canning	52
The Tired Old Man	Harry Brookes	53
The Bittern	Neil Middleton	54
This Beautiful World	Farzana Baz	55
A Poem	Stella Rose Haylett	56
Christmas Thoughts	Irene G Corbett	57
Rockham Bay	David William Buxton	58
Invisible Picture	Anna Maria Shenton	59
Natural Beauty	Daniel Roper	60
Lonely Life	Nora Smith	61
Working Blues	Diane Birtwisle	62
Might As Well Be A Fly	Janet Hannan	63
Maybe	Margaret Nicol	64
The Spring	Jean Jukes	65
State Of The World	Karin Clarkson	66
Autumn Morning	Margaret Thomas	67
Body And Soul Reunited	Vanessa Rivington	68
Christmas Eve	Evette Robinson	69
Potato Harvesting	J Faulkner	70
Don't They Know	Audrey P S Williams	71
Where Angels Call Home	Marie Ness	72
Be Graceful	Barry Fletcher	73

School Days	M B Such	74
Our Fireplace	Vernon L Hawks	75
The Lane	Marjorie V Lewis	76
A Cherrie Little Dittie	Mary Simmonds	77
Pleasing Myself	Lyn Round	78
Clickety Click	Iain M MacLeod	79
To The Rescue On The Western Lawns	Kenneth James Brown	80
Rings On Their Fingers	F W Bowman	81
The Four Seasons	G Bullman	82
Walkies	Norma Benstead	83
Cry Within A Dream	K W Butler	84
Panorama Panorama	Len Beddow	85
Rhyme And Reason	Jean Acott	86
On Your Wedding Day	Pauline Clark	87
Ask Yourself	D Rochester	88
The Cotswolds	Grace Graham	89
The Hardest Thing Of All	Anne Horne	90
I See	John Cameron	91
Hopes	K R Frost	92
Double Trouble	Lynn Morley	93
The Haunted Mill	Carol Fay Clarke	94
Untitled	J Hudspeth	95
The Housewife And The Salesman	D Jeffery	96
Why?	Emma Jones	97
Telly Addicts	Charles Robinson	98
Torquay	April Barry	99
The Telescope	Edward M Shipsey	101
Beckoning Of The Seasons	F G Challenger	102
Summer Ride	June Misson	103
Happy Sunshine Hours	P E Langton	104
Millionaire	Sylvia Salisbury	105
The Loss Of A Child	Hilary Peck	106
Higger Tor	Dilys Paulson	107
Untitled	Hilda Coe	108
The River Walk	Terrence McIntyre	109
Springtime	F M Joynes	110

Christmas Cheer	Doris West	111
Spectacles . . .	Jean Osborne	112
Dark Thoughts	Connie Barker	113
An Old Man's Memories	Sylvia Needham	114
Moments In Time	James Strawbridge	115
Chobie Dainty	Lawson Phillips	116
Time	W T Longman	117
Prairie Farm	Kay Gilbert	118
The Biggest Gift	J B A Roe	119
The Little Old Lady	Valerie Browning	121
Prince	Shirley Travis	122

MY HUSBAND

My husband is so forgetful, he really exasperates me,
I shall be grey before much longer, it's plain for all to see.
You remind him of things, oh, again and again
He simply forgets - and then tries to explain.
I loose my temper - not as that's much good
His head I declare must be made of wood.
I ask him to do just one little task
But oh dear no, he will not grasp.
I write things down, in black and white
The paper goes with him, that's alright.
But low and behold when he arrives back
The papers he's forgot - I'll give him the sack.

S Barker

TRYING TO SLIM

An apple for dinner, a pear for tea,
I'm really trying to get slim you see.
I'll cut down on sugar and watch my weight,
And turn my nose up at those fresh cream cakes.
I'll keep off the chips and try to be brave,
And remind myself I'm losing weight.
But it takes so long to lose this weight,
And my plates empty and my stomach's in a state.
It's not so easy to lose this weight.
I must be re-educated in what I eat,
And one day my figure will look such a treat.

Val Roberts

MY MYSTERY MAN

My mystery man is simply gorgeous!
He is made of fluffy wool,
Who keeps me warm in the cold.
He is a blue bell
Who can charm any red rose,
But, his heart is a star
Which cannot be caught.
He is a juicy orange
Who likes to share his juice with another orange!
He is a big comfy bed
Who gives me a smooth night
And, he is a big fluffy dog
Who shares his basket with a small furry cat.
He is the warm wind
Who holds me tight
And, is a hot meal
Who keeps me warm inside.
He is a white wine
Who tastes very sweet,
And is a glass frame
Containing many happy memories.
He is a big soft blanket
Who wraps himself tightly round me.
He is the colour mustard
For it simply suits him,
And is a carrot
Which cannot be bitten in to.
And of course,
He is the most romantic piece of music
Who I fell in love with
        The moment I laid eyes on.

Rahmanara Chowdhury

3

ANSWER TO YOUR QUESTION

Write about the area where you live,
So what impression can I give?
This is a complex for the retired.
So I hope this ditty will be admired.

We have a warden who wends her way,
Around to each bungalow every day
Asking us if we've had a good night
And to see if everyone is alright,
The milkman has been, and the
Grocery van's due
They're very helpful, it's everyone's view.

Out on a trip, glassworks today,
Three pounds each we have had to pay.
Lawrence the writer he came from here
We're getting quite famous and
Full of good cheer.
I've had one poem published
I'm over the moon,
A second effort is out very soon.
To all my friends in Eastwood I'll say,
I hope to be famous like
Lawrence one day.

Alice Stapleton

4

DAY DUSK AND DAWN

Meadows full of summer flowers
Cows are grazing the day light hours
As dusk creeps over the rocky hills
Machines close down in the distant mills.
Bats fly out of the old church roof,
The owl on the gravestone doesn't give a hoot
The dormouse returns at the break of day
Curls up tight in his nest of hay.

Marion Bramley

MOODS

Quietly moving through the night,
Silence, waiting for dawn light,
The wind soft and gentle blows
Where it comes from no-one knows,
It travels over land and out to sea,
Then impatient to go on a spree,
Pushing and hurrying, moving so fast
After the hurt and damage - settled at last.
Then with a whisper and a sigh
It has gone, quick to tire
The dawn breaks and silence once more,
What made it angry? And what for.
And like life, sometimes gentle and quiet,
Other times angry and full of fright.
So one thing at a time and gently so,
Just like the wind - anger quick to go.

Hilda Whyman

HEALTHY DIET

Doctors say we must not eat
Anything that's really sweet.
Added salt, no not ever
It's bad for our blood pressure.
Apple pie in a sea of cream
Has become only a dream.
A lovely big, juicy steak
We are told is a mistake.
Eggs, pate and soft cheeses
Are we know, full of diseases.
An apple a day keeps the doctor away
No! It's bad for us, or so they say.
Don't drink whisky or table wine
For your liver will show the sign.
And they say we must not smoke
'Cos the damage will be no joke.
Even water isn't good for you
Containing chemicals, bacteria too.
What to eat is really a puzzle
I think I'll give up and have a guzzle.

Gill Cannon

THE FIRST SNOW

Rising slowly from her bed,
She rubbed her eyes and shook her head.
Outside, the north winds cry was loud,
As it swept the sky in a dark grey shroud.

Stumbling blindly to the window,
Her eyes still tired and slow,
She gazed out upon a white, wintry scene.
Not a single inch broken by a blade of green.

A blanket of snow lay gleaming, as far as the eye could see,
Inviting happy children to come on a sledging spree.
Icicles hang trembling from the trees,
Suspended in time until the freeze.
The first snow of winter is here,
For the young at heart it will raise a cheer.

The snow brings quiet all around,
Only a solitary robin makes a sound.
Bold little red chested fellow, they say,
A lonely creature on a bleak cold day.

As she surveys the day with discontent,
Her body old and slightly bent,
The cold pervades the window panes,
Sending shivers through her veins.

There was a time when years ago,
When she would hurry out into the snow.
Building castles made of ice,
And brave the cold at any price.

Her youth all spent with no regret,
As time goes past she'll not forget.
Back to the comfort of a soft warm bed,
The childhood memories still fresh in her head.

Madeline Derrham

GOING FOR A WALK

I walked along the riverside
On a perfect summer's day
But so had many others
And the grass was worn away

Years ago I would have been alone
With no litter or tin cans
That was before the motor car
Public loos and ice cream vans

But perhaps I'm being selfish
For everyone has a right to view
The beautiful English countryside
Not just the privileged few

So I'll look to the other side
For there's no pathway there
And I'll see how it used to be
Before I had to share

Wild flowers grow in profusion
The grass is tall and lush
Ducks guiding their families
Safely through reed and rush

Yellow wagtails, water voles
All nature on display
Giving pleasure to everyone
On a perfect summer's day.

Rosalie Upton

REFLECTIONS

As I sit in my chair and wonder
What life has in store for me
One half says I wish I knew
The other half says let it be.
Why worry about the future
Let's live from day to day
Enjoy each hour that's given us
And go merrily on our way
So don't try to see the future
You might not like what you see
So why worry about what lies ahead
When your mind could be fancy free.

Eileen Neal

FRANCESCHA

Francescha always wets the bed
She's just as tough as a piece of lead
She always kicks and pulls your hair
Her skin is as soft as a juicy pear
Francescha loves her little dolls
She swings and slides along the poles
Just like she does with our breakfast bowls
How she loves to play outside
She thinks it's better than our slide
I know she likes all our trolls
She puts them into dirty holes
She also draws inside my books
She hangs them on my curtain hooks
She likes two sugars
She said you buggers
She is so sloppy
I think she's potty.

M Babbington

MUSIC EVERYWHERE

There's music in the trees,
If you stand still and listen -
Softly on the summer breeze,
Melodies floating down from heaven.

There's music in the tinkling stream
As it meanders on its way
Through verdant pastures green,
To where the river waters play.

There's music in a blackbird's song
As he welcomes in the dawn,
And his mate in her shrill treble responds
To tell us a new day is born.

Elsie Gadsby

THE OLD HOUSE

The windows of the house no longer gleamed, the sparkle in them
gone
It awaited the fate which God had deemed, and no one could save it
from
Once it had stood so straight and proud in the days of its early youth
The frame so strong which now was bowed, as it realised the truth

It recalled the times of distant days, when happiness abounded
Love enveloped the work and strife and a family was founded
It watched them grow with motherly pride in the things which they'd
achieve
And it felt an ache, it tried to hide when they finally came to leave.

They returned, these children for one last look at at part of them now
dead
And what they found was a long closed book whose words they
hadn't read
But in their dreams the past returned, to make them understand
All the things which had been learned, within that childhood land

They soon recalled forgotten years from the corners of their mind
And they found again the childish fears, which always had entwined
They felt the overpowering gloom, of night and unlit stairs
They heard the whispers from the room, which long ago was there.

They sensed the old, familiar smell, of rooms kept just for best
Rooms where parties raged like hell, or the dead were laid to rest
They saw again the gypsy child who lived along the street
The old men from the lodging house, surrounded by defeat

They heard the ghostly, fluttering wings, of pigeons overheard
And the kindly voice of Grandpa, as he put them to their bed
The memories came flooding back of friends no longer there
And they could only mourn the lack and loss of something rare

But its life was surely not in vain, it had served its purpose well
When happy memories remain, in the hearts of those who dwell,
For they spoke with gratitude and pride of years which had long gone
They knew the house could never die, while its presence lingered on.

Gwendolyn Cameron

ON REFLECTION

I went back and looked in a mirror,
I looked in a mirror - what did I see!
I looked in that mirror some twenty years on,
And the face that I see is not me.
The mirror the same, dance hall the same,
Young girls and boys still act the same game.
Musicians still play upon the same stage,
But the tempo and beat is not the same age.
Returning to haunts from twenty years past,
I did for the first time and surely the last.

Barbara Gundry-White

FOREVER

The joy I feel at nature's wondrous things,
The fresh beauty that spring always brings.
The birds so busy the trees in bloom,
It will go on forever, we all assume.
It makes me sad, I want it to last,
I want it for the future, as well as the past.
The earth and nature, so finely tuned,
We tip the scale, we find it doomed.

From insect to animals and superior man,
All have reason in God's wonderful plan.
Kindness and caring we will get the best,
Carry on as we are, we'll all be distressed.
From Radioactive waste to pesticide sprays,
We sicken our earth and limit our days.

Anne Chaloner

SUMMER'S SONG

Soft the sound of Summer's song
By balmy breezes borne along,
Poplars rustling like a sigh
And buzzing bees in grass waist high
Gather gold from cowslips shy.

Oh! With what joy skylarks rise,
Soaring in the azure skies,
Whilst far away in sheltered vale
The cuckoo tells his timeless tale
To lowing cattle in the dale.

Butterflies on painted wing
Kiss each flower, crickets sing,
And blackbirds to their fledglings croon,
Joining Nature's perfect tune,
Unmistakably 'tis *June*!

Jean Graham

THE SIGNS

So quiet and still in my bed I lie,
Looking through the window at the deep dark sky.
It's sprinkled with stars that glitter and shine,
Some in a pattern, some in a line.
The moon is out and how it does glow,
But it's on its back, *that's a sign* of snow.

The sounds of the night so weird and strange,
A dog outside howling, as if it has mange.
The wind through the eaves is puffing and blowing,
As though it's a cow that is mooing and bowing.
The sound in the distance, I think it's a train,
You know what they say, *that's a sign* of rain.

There's something there now I didn't see before,
A flashing red light across the sky it does soar,
My mind it plays tricks and gives me a fright.,
It looks like a flying saucer hovering in the night
Oh, it's only a plane, my skin has gone creepy
My eyes grow heavy *that's a sign* that I'm sleepy.

I close my eyes, its darker still now,
My mind still active, to sleep I don't know how.
I think of the plane that gave me a fright,
Where will it be going, on this dark night.
Will there be red skies to greet it in the morning,
They say *that's a sign* of a bad day dawning.

Deeper and deeper into the night my thoughts seem,
I turn from the windows in search of a dream.
The gold of the stars, the purple dark sky,
The red of the sun, when morning is nigh.
The colours they mingle, in my mind they get stuck.
A rainbow appears, *that's a sign* of good luck.

Janet Wainwright

WISHES AND DREAMS

If I could wish a dream come true
We'd go on a journey - just me and you.
There, all your troubles, big and small
Would fade away to nothing at all

I'd wish you linger in a lush meadow sweet
Fragrant clover and daisies profuse at your feet
On a balmy evening - a birds soft refrain
Predicting the fall of the warm summer rain.

You would ride on a rainbow, pluck stars from the skies
Feel the butterfly breath of a baby's soft sighs
Touch filigree snowflakes before they alight
On mountains and fields on a cold frosty night

I'd wish you had wings to swiftly glide
O'er misty valleys deep and wide
Or to swim like a mermaid in tropical seas
Ride the crest of a wave in a tingling breeze

And when you felt ready to lay down to sleep
I'd wish you soft mattresses one hundred deep
Your tired head would sink so deep in your pillow
Thanks to the down from the soft pussy willow

I wish I could make all these dreams come true
But my special dream - and I wish it for you
I'd lay you down in an enchanted dell
And bid the fairies make you well.

For Meresia with love.

Barbara Gearing

A HOLIDAY TO REMEMBER

We sat on the train, Grandpa and I
Talking of years that have just slipped by

When the children were home, there was no time to spare
Tending these precious gifts from God in our care

Now they have grown and gone away
Still following God's teaching, we're proud to say

Journey's end, we're met at the station
By two children of the next generation

Hugs and kisses, joy fills our hearts
With love for this family of which we are part

Days in the park, days by the sea
Days in the garden, just sitting lazily

Games to play, shouts of glee,
We'd forgotten what fun children can be

Sunday at Church, how uplifting to share
Praises to God through Hymns and Prayer

Our holiday over, our stay at an end
And homeward now our way we must wend

'Mid tearful farewells, what lifts the gloom?
'We love you Grandma and Grandpa, come back soon.'

Annelyn Jax

THE LOVE WITHIN
Dedicated to Helen Bilics

My love is pure beauty,
The sapphire in the sky,
The waterfall that cascades,
Sharing itself with life.
She fills my life with meaning
By caring from the start,
I feel as though an Angel
Has touched deep inside my heart.
She's as perfect as a rainbow,
During April days,
As beautiful, as sunshine,
I bathe in golden rays.
Equal to the flowers
That paint the open fields,
Her scent a rose-like fragrance,
Her face the shining moon.
Enchanting and attractive,
She's a marvellous portrait,
She uses magic love powder,
To help us seal our fate,
Forever we will be together,
And never will we part,
For only to be separated
Would only break my heart.

Philip May

WHO'D BE A MOTHER AT CHRISTMAS TIME?

Christmas for me is about celebrations
And being reacquainted with relations
With people I see but only once a year
When they all come to meet around here
I take their coats, and I offer them drinks
Whilst they go about renewing old links
I play the role of the perfect host
Whilst cooking veg, and the turkey roast
In the kitchen I listen to what goes on
The moaning, bickering, laughter and fun

Susie's given a present, and begins to holler
'I would never be seen dead in that colour!'
Tommy is crying that he hasn't had a go
Since hubby's been playing with his nintendo
Uncle Frank shouts he can't hear the telly
Whilst Uncle Joe argues with Auntie Nelly
Grandpa is getting sloshed, Grandma is getting mad
And Tommy cries yet again, 'Lets have a go, Dad!'
And every now and then, someone calls my name
'Could you . . . .', 'how about . . . ', and more of the same

Evening has arrived, and I'm feeling rather glad
Everyone tells me what a great time they've had
When everybody's gone, I start the washing up
I then begin to give the kitchen floor a good mop
I empty the ashtrays, and I clear up the mess
For when it comes to cleaning, hubby's hopeless
Finally when I think I've done more than enough
Hubby then says 'Why don't you sit down, love?'
I then think to myself, collapsed in a chair
'Thank goodness Christmas is only once a year!'

Loraine Jane Banner

THE SONG

The tap, tap, tap, on my window pane,
      From that tall green tree outside.
I'd tried for hours to go to sleep,
      But no good, my eyes were open wide.

I could see the dark clouds scurrying by,
      As I lay there snug and warm.
But something wouldn't let me sleep,
      Like an invisible ghostly form.

I lay there and I listened hard,
      To a soft moaning in the trees.
With now and then a piercing shriek,
      That made my blood stream freeze.

Then suddenly I realised all,
      No ghost who had long since sinned.
Those piercing shrieks and gentle moans,
      Were the night songs of the wind.

A B Hughes

THE MAGICIAN

He could do magic, the Conjuror's art.
He smiled and he mended her broken heart.

With sleight of hand, he placed the ring
Upon her finger, her heart did sing.

Like Svengali, he hypnotised.
She was under his spell. His love she prized.

She became his assistant and helped on the stage.
She was part of the act, like the dove in the cage.

His tricks deceived her; she didn't guess
That, as time went by, he loved her less.

The warning voice, from her mind she banished.
When the curtain came down, the magician had vanished!

Linda Blakey

CHANGING SEASONS

Autumn with fingers long and gold
Has touched the summer leaves
And soon their fragile loveliness
Will scatter in the breeze.

Cold frosts will come, and change the green
Through yellow into gold
And capture in each fleeting glance
A glory to behold.

And so it is with human life
Midsummer green soon past.
The autumn glow and winter chill
Comes on us all at last.

So make the most of days that come
Of pleasure take your fill
Then every day will give to you
A golden daffodil.

Elsie Anderson

DICKIE DANDELION

My dandelion's called Dick he can run very quick
Makes me quite sick my dandelion mate.

No need for house training never does any staining
Wants out when it is raining my dandelion friend.
Does not need feeding just an occasional weeding
Got him as a seedling my dandelion pal.
Always does as he oughter likes drinks of cold water
Plays a lot with my daughter my dandelion mate.
One day I did cry I thought he would die
Covered in greenfly my dandelion friend.
I gave him a spray four times that day
Those bugs fell away my dandelion pal.
He began to change it was so strange
Petals in disarrange my dandelion mate.
Now he is fluffy like a little puppy
All over very scruffy my dandelion friend.
I realise indeed now he is a weed
That has turned to seed my dandelion pal.
So now with a sigh we say our goodbye
It is time he must fly my dandelion mate.
Goodbye my dandelion, goodbye.

D A Watson

MY FOUR FOOTED FRIEND

'A silly cat
Who can't talk back?
How silly you sound!
My friend - this mouse on my mat
Is her way of saying
Thank you.

A silly cat
Who can't talk back?
Her kneading paws,
Her tear wet fur and purring weight
Were lent because she couldn't say
I'm sorry.

A psychic cat
Makes your chatter silly.
But I don't mind.
You are my friend and so is she.
I can tell you my highs and lows . . .
But Suki isn't like that
She *knows*!

Mary Fry

ME

I think I'm getting boring,
Too middle class, I mean,
I drive a nice red rover,
I always keep her clean.
Although I've got much more now,
Than my parents ever had,
Why does life seem so pointless?
Why does it make me sad?
Whatever happened to my roots.
My working class ideas,
Must keep up with the Jones's
No mortgage in arrears.
I was weaned on toast and dripping,
And home-made jam for tea.
Whatever am I doing here?
Is this the life for me?

Charles Hunter

SEASIDE OUT OF SEASON

The blinds are down on all the stalls
The deck chairs are stacked away
There are no children on the beach
It's raining, and the sky is grey

The fairgrounds closed down and deserted
Like a ghost town waiting there
All the rides are still and eerie
There is litter everywhere

There lingers still the smell of popcorn
Candyfloss and fish and chips
I can almost see the children there
With ketchup on their lips

The gift shops look neglected
Selling things the people didn't buy
Plastic buckets, spades and paddles
It almost makes me want to cry

The little train is at a standstill
No more rides, it's in its stall
Like a giant caterpillar
A green tarpaulin covers all

The Punch and Judy hut is shuttered
Boarded up from winter's storm
The small arcades are almost empty
Just a few boys keeping warm

It's getting dark now as I leave
The lights illuminate the pier
Reflections of a summer gone
Reminders of a winter here.

Joy Pickering

LIFE'S STAGE

All the world's a stage
    People merely players,
The curtains drawn the stage is set,
    And yet,
The stars are in the sky.

We see these pictures almost every day,
    In the papers or in the news.
With sadness or a smile
    Some may last a while
        Or fade away.

Maybe some day, another time
    For fortune's gain or fame,
Their stairway to those stars will climb.

Some tragic or notorious
    Their prestige portrayed inglorious,
When in the end the curtains fall,
    We may then bow to them all.

S V Smy

STRANGER IN THE NIGHT

I woke up frightened
In the middle of the night
If you live by yourself
You'll understand my plight

My body tensed
My face went red
Someone is beside me
Right here on the bed

I sat bolt upright
And fumbled for the light
I turned around to see
Who gave me such a fright

I quickly realised
What the raider was about
But then chaps. Let's face it
I couldn't throw her out.

Frank McCabe

MY LOVE IS LIKE A RED RED DOZE

Shall I compare you to a deep depression over Iceland?
Gale Force Wind in the Willows,
Granite Face on the Pillows
Hailstones on the Hacienda
Winter Solstice in Samoa.
Snow Ploughs out in California
Freezing Fog in Abu Dhabi
Under Insured in Ethiopia
Black Ice in Uganda.
Freeze-up in Fiji
Breathalyzed in Bangalore
Write-off in the Wilderness
Towed Away in Tasmania.

Catherine Nair

REASON TO LIVE (FOR MIA)

It's long the road that I've travelled
It's many a tear that I've cried
I'm beginning to see the sunlight again
It's there when I look in your eyes

My heart has been heavy and weary
It struggled sometimes to pull through
But now that I've found it a resting place
It longs to be cared for by you

You're the girl that has made me so happy
And I do thank the Lord up above
That into my life he has sent you
For to give to me someone to love

For if love is all that you're asking
Then it's love that I promise to give
And I'll cherish each moment I'm with you
As it's you who gives me reason to live.

D McKeown

SUNDAY TEA

Sunday tea was something special
Long ago when I was small
Seated round the big oak table
When Aunts and Uncles came to call
Tablecloth of Irish linen
Embroidered with such loving care
Silver teapot, best bone china
Dishes piled with tempting fare
Sandwiches of egg or salmon
Buttered scones with home-made jam
Lettuce picked from down the garden
Alongside plates of Yorkshire ham
Macaroons and shortbread fingers
Gingerbread and seedy cake
All made in our cosy kitchen
At the weekly Friday bake
Pleasant chatter, time to linger
Life lived at a gentler pace
Now we're all in such a hurry
As if pursuing one, long race.

Sheila Leheup

ODE TO DUSTY

My little black vagabond
Teeth claws and fur, playful in love,
My little black vagabond I watch you
From afar, I talked to you softly
And you had an answer
What were you saying my little friend?
I did not know, I could not walk
In your feline talk.
Friends came and parted in the years
And enemies ate into my soul
But you remained and did not take.

My little black vagabond
With a life to lead as full as any worldly man,
Yes you protected us both, our love
Our crown, our crest, our sisterhood
My gallant little hero
Romances you failed, lost and won
And offspring,
A hundred little babes.
Echo through the county.

My little black vagabond
Where are you now?
Yes I hear you, watching from afar
Teeth claws and fur, playful in love.

Jane S Simpson

35

SPRINGING IN THE RAIN

Standing
Watching
In the street
Running
Water
Wets my feet
Raindrops
Falling
From the sky
Cars and
Buses
Driving by
Laughing
As the
Puddles grow
Jumping
Splashing
Waters flow
Raining
Stops and
My heart sighs
Sunlight
Returning
To the skies.

Sarah Maycock

MAY TO DECEMBER

Our meeting in the month of May
Induced my heart to pound.
By June I was on gossamer wings
My feet had left the ground

And in July there was a bond
Between yourself and I.
By August we were sure
That we would never break the tie.

September we were still in love
As well we might well be.
October was the month of tears
With sad reality.

November brought us down to earth
Like rain that comes in showers.
December was the month we knew
Love was no longer ours.

Phyllis Harvey

VANQUISHED DREAMS

A hard life had the wartime mother's
When all their kids were small,
When husbands were called to duty
To win freedom for us all.

The heartaches must have been many,
The problems hard to surmount,
But courage, faith, and unity,
And true friendship, helped them out.

They went without to feed their brood,
They borrowed, shared, and cared,
They stood together side by side,
Their hopes and dreams compared.

A better life, a better world,
Is what they thought there'd be,
How many now I wonder
Are disillusioned by what they see?

For now they feel abandoned,
Their fears are all to clear,
The dreams and hopes they cherished
Paid by blood and tears, was dear.

They still have that wartime pride
That made them heroines of their day,
They now fight again for justice,
For their rights, and for fair play.

Jean Little

FIRESIDE EYELIDS

Let's both unravel
by an all night pile
of firewood.
Sleep under night's carpet
lose our voices in a
babbling brook. Laugh about
lost dreams.
Forget what we believed.
Fall loose and helpless
in the night's open chambers.
Float safely on
a smoke raft. In a water tight
moon stream.

Michael Coey

REFLECTIONS FROM A SILVER KETTLE

I can see a picture of a person, thinking in retrospect
The mists of time. The magic of memory is conjured forth,
And the person though sitting is running through a
Sunbathed wooded glade. The white shorts are easily noticeable,
So too are the plimsolls and the short cropped hair.

What a pity! Even though I try, I find that I cannot hold
the image. Alas! It has gone.

Here I find myself again, amid the physical austerity of
Life. The enchantment of youth remaining, only as a clouded
reflection in the mind.

A C J Williams

EN HIVER

Smoke plumed lazily from the chimney top
Frost rimed, heavy on the windows,
   Outside, snow, glistening under the
Cold stare of the moon.
Cast a mantle of white across the land
Trees, starkly etched, with tops of snow,
Stood, like bewigged judges of long ago
         Inside firelight, danced
Flickering shadows, round the darkening room
And peace, like a comforting hand cradled
         This land.

Peter Read

THE TEARDROP

A little boy with a badly grazed knee.
A sad little face gazing up at me.
A warm little body pressed close to mine
Willing that I make everything fine.

And as I looked down I saw trembling there.
On a curly eyelash that matched his hair
The most perfect teardrop I ever did see
Which even as I watched was gone from me.

Like a first snowflake full of beauty profound
Only to vanish as it touches the ground,
So the teardrop rolled down his rosy face
Just like the snowflake to vanish without trace.

If only it were possible for me to imprison
This perfect teardrop in a little glass prism
There for all time for me to see
To awake a memory of a little cut knee.

When you are grown and gone away
I could keep it to gaze at every day
Part of your childhood then gone from me
Part of the child that was given to me.

Dorothy N Davies

42

I HEAR YOU CRYING

Returning to the fold,
Far away from the cold,
I hear you crying,
From the wilderness.

Outcast you were,
Brother you are now,
Here in the face,
Of war famine and hunger.

Aren't you glad,
You came back
We salute and greet you,
As if you've been always here

I hear you crying,
In the wilderness
Crying to be saved
From all that's wrong in the world.

So don't return
To life of mystery and violence
Always here to remain,
The perfect entitlement.

Mike Vukasinovic

43

ALWAYS

You came along when I was sad you didn't look all that bad
I wasn't sure what you were after was it just fun and laughter
This was the second time for me it wasn't easy as you could see
I was very badly hurt before when he left me and walked out the door
You promised to love me for for all your life and one day I would be
your wife
I had two boys from day one they now call you dad and you call them
son
We have a son his not that old his our Dan Dan our piece of gold
We are still not man and wife but I know I have a family for all my life
We have been together for seven happy years you took away my
biggest fears
You kept your promise you have taken care of me and everyone
around us can see
You gave me hope and happiness that those three little words
cannot express
I hope this poem helps you to see you mean all the world to me.

Jane McGarry

44

DEATH OF A TROUBLED SOUL

A powerless hand sweeps unseen through crystal waters.
Energy flows like static in the air.
Waves lap the shore, the air, the mind.
Pin pricks in the dark, sharp thoughts in the air.
A body floats on pulsing water.
Rhythmic beats of heart and wave combine.
Lethargic memories dance through empty hands.
Freedom claims the empty painful life.
Wraps itself around the limbs and flesh.
Pulling ever deeper,
Deeper into clearer water,
Deeper still into a sharper understanding.
Into a state of everlasting peace.

Samantha Ambrose

LOVE

When we were young, and love was young
Our intertwined lives just begun
We loved with passion till, passion spent
We lay to rest, our hearts content
To procreate in perfect form,
The evidence of our life's love born
To nurture, cherish, Love and learn
The nature of our love's heart burn
To raise with pleasure, pride and maze
With wonder on our love's child gaze
With passing years to yearn again
The love we still kept to contain
The seed of yet another child
To once again become beguiled
And parenthood again to know
To proudly raise and proudly show
To raise again across the years
Present an adult to his peers
As down life's flowing river go
The many years that we will know
The good, the bad, the moribund
The richness of life's natural fund
The love we had, has quietened, slept
Occasions roused, but tired, and kept
Within a closely shuttered grate
Has stifled long in mourning state
Oh! That we could be young again
And passion's fire need not contain
Rekindle once again the coals
And bum within from twining souls
Our bodies merging, yet to love
As we had done, when we were young, when we were young

This outer shell age o'er has crept
Is not the me my mind has kept
For now I'll state again, once more
Inside I'm still just twenty four.

Alexander

SEASONS COME AND GO

The seasons come the seasons go
And with the winter comes the snow
Covering the ground with white
Winter darkness replaces summer light
The length of summer days has gone
It's now short days for everyone
It takes its toll on young and old
The warmth replaced by damp and cold
The fruits of summer are no more
We have to live off what's in store
For anything that has to live
The winter hasn't much to give
Wildlife struggles to stay alive
Only the strongest can survive
As daylight hours start to get longer
The winter cold starts to get stronger
When February comes to an end
Spring is only round the bend
Winter might have its last fling
But it always loses to the spring
But after spring just like before
The months of plenty come once more
Some birds and beast have met their fate
Alas for them it came too late
But life goes on as we all know
The seasons they still come and go.

David A Howard

PASTURES NEW

A kind old friend is going away,
> Not long now to the moving day.
All his possessions stored and packed,
> With plenty of memories still intact.

Memories of a bygone life,
> One he shared with a dear, dear, wife.
A grieving time with face so sad,
> Longing for the one he had.

His canine friend has left him too,
> A nice old dog with eyes so true.
I wonder why this has to be,
> It always, always puzzles me.

I am going to miss this friend of mine,
> And will think of him from time to time,
Shall miss his chat, and, friendly smile,
> But will pause and think, once in a while.

Of the tales he told, and the folks, he knew,
> And the laughs we had - quite a few.
New paths to tread, new faces to see,
> I hope he will, remember me.

I have a gift, he gave with pleasure,
> Something for me to tend and treasure,
But happy days, I hope and pray,
> For this dear old friend, are here to stay.

E K Bainbridge

NIGHT AT THE FAIR

Assortment of lights reflect
An excited face in groups or pairs
Music swirls throughout brisk air
Organised crowds set alight lively fair

Carnival wheel lit with screens
Reaching the hop sounds slightly dim
Starry sky seems so near but far
Retiring downward amusements ring loud

Additive smells capture fun night
Hunger sets in, horde's amply fed
Candyfloss, hot-dogs, apples painted syrupy red
Appetites met ends visit on open fair.

A Jones

TEDDY'S DILEMMA

It had been raining all day when Lauren came to stay,
We were all sat around wondering what games to play.
It was soon decided to play hide 'n seek,
'You're on, Grandad, close your eyes and don't peep.'
Lauren goes off with Lassie and Blaze to hide,
Her dolls and Teddy scampering behind.

Lauren creeps behind the curtains
Leaving her tiny shoes sticking out.
Lassie just managed to squeeze in behind the couch,
Blaze shot through the open back door,
Grabs Teddy with his head,
Then buries him like a bone behind Grandad's toolshed,
Blaze dives under her blanket she uses for her bed.

'Coming, ready or not,' Grandad's heard to shout,
He soon spots Lassie for her tail is sticking out.
His attention is now drawn to the curtains,
Points to Lauren, a tittering little bump.
The friends all look around, but Teddy can't be found.

Blaze rescues Teddy, but he's now in a terrible mess,
Grandad thinks a warm bath will be for the best.
Teddy is wrapped in a towel and given a warm cup of tea.
He slowly recovers looking all shy and meek,
Says, 'It's great fun when playing hide 'n seek.

K Pendlebury

HOLLY

Was it a bird that brought you
When you were a tiny seed?
And tucked you into my garden
A kind and caring deed.

I'm glad you caught my attention
Your tiny leaves sparkling green,
Reflecting the rays of sunlight
So prettily, had to be seen.

I know your name is Holly
And in time will grow quite tall,
So perhaps I'd better transplant you
A little further away from the wall.

And now I'll continue weeding,
But not quite so ruthlessly,
In case there are other orphans
In need of care from me.

Amelia Canning

THE TIRED OLD MAN

A weary old man stops to rest on our hill
He's struggled through life, and he's struggling still
With his ashen grey face, and his eyes looking sad
The old man whom I see is really my dad

He's helped to make steel, he's helped to dig coal
He fought for his country, then signed on the dole
If the belief, *Hard work equals riches*, means anything
This old man should have lived like a King

In spite of his pain, his hardships, his labours
His wealth is his family, his friends and his neighbours
As he looks in my face he gives me a smile
I'm one of his kids who've made it worth while.

Harry Brookes

THE BITTERN

A secretive, stealthy Bittern strode across the reeds,
Reeds tall and thin encompassed and enclosed him,
Adam's ale ran among the bed of reeds,
Zephyr depressed the elongated stem and tufty tips

The tall tawny torso of that Bittern stood bolt upright
And emitted an almighty blare *Boom! Boom!* it called.
Seasonal male mating rituals were about to materialise,
As he called, the Bittern perceived that prey was advancing.

Crack! the bayonet-like beak plunged into the depths of the water.
The fish fought to be released from the hunter's grip.
Ripples on the surface came more vigorously as the fish
twisted and turned to try and attain autonomy

The Bittern erected its crown, unlocked its neb and
Consumed its meal whole. The fish fell to its doom.
Our Bittern waded across a gully into its own bailiwick
And descended onto a bed of withe.

The day had concluded.

Neil Middleton

THIS BEAUTIFUL WORLD

I wake up in the morning,
I hear the birds singing and people yawning.
Then I look out the window to see
How beautiful this world can be.

But deep out there it's bright and blue,
The sun is shining and I feel great.
I get out of bed and I go down to
Enjoy this beautiful world.

Farzana Baz

A POEM

The seaside and the countryside
Are fascinating wondrous places
With sand and sea and shells
And lambs, skylarks, wheat and corn
Let the children roam by the sea
Or in the English countryside green
Help them Dear God to cherish
Our little Island home
Let them play on clean sand
And through meadows of wild
Flowers and grass rich and cool and green
Let them wander through our
Countryside and rich and healthy grow
Help them one and all from prince
To beggar small help them to love one another
And our little Island home.

Stella Rose Haylett

CHRISTMAS THOUGHTS

Christmas comes, with all its cheer
Bringing thoughts of those
We hold so dear
Be they far, or be they near
Our thoughts go back, to childhood days
Of Christmas long ago
Candles on the tree, all aglow
Frost in the air, dragging the tree, through snow
Childhood days, full of joy
Without a word, we plucked the bird
Without a sound, listen! Is that Santa's Reindeer
Over the roofs, or on the ground
With wide eyed wonder, our faces pressed
Against the window pane
'Santa won't come, until your fast asleep!'
Mother was heard, to explain
The innocence of childhood, let it still remain
Christmas is a happy time, a family time
With gifts, underneath the tree
But we remember, those we've loved
Whom no longer, we can see
Happy times, of Christmas past
Carols in the snow, making feet and fingers glow
Log fires, chestnuts, mistletoe
A baby in a manger lay
Born for us, on Christmas day
So rejoice, fill our hearts with love
For Christmas now, and long ago
A gift from, Heaven above.

Irene G Corbett

ROCKHAM BAY

The aged cliff of Rockham Bay
Enfolds the restless waves
Their silver crests lie gently there
Against her golden hair.

Her ancient cap festooned with flowers
Caressed by scented winds
Her guiding paths and ports of rest,
A haven for the blest.

When I have travelled stormy seas,
When rocks have barred my way,
When fear and doubt obscure the shore,
I need your love the more.

My thoughts of you enfold me too
As the cliffs around the bay
Embrace the waves with rocky arm
Bringing peace and lasting calm.

David William Buxton

INVISIBLE PICTURE

Beneath the mountain lies a meadow of greens,
Rich in its colour, with spectacular scenes,
Covered with raindrops that fell from the sky,
This picture of truth, which can't tell a lie.

Black clouds where gathering, on the mountains peak,
A storm from nowhere, it must be a freak,
Smoky filled sun rays, bursting with rain,
Beaming so gloriously, to the picture's gain.

Peace and tranquillity, a place to escape,
Miles of freedom, not a hint of red tape,
Endless hills of velvet, all roll into one,
Its panoramic views, are second to none.

Close your eyes tightly as tight as can be,
You'll feel the breeze blowing, just like me,
Captured is this beauty, locked inside your head,
The invisible picture, your imaginations been fed.

Anna Maria Shenton

NATURAL BEAUTY

Here I am lying awake.
Looking into the nearest lake
A natural beauty is what you are
I'm looking to find the nearest star

I just want to fly away
For some reason I feel I'm here to stay
I know the reason for why I'm here
Is to be with you forever my dear.

Your sweet soul is what I sought
But life for me seems so short
That red rose will last forever
As long as we will be together.

Daniel Roper

LONELY LIFE

Oh it is a lonely life
To live the part of a drunkard's wife
My old man's out every night
Loves to drink and loves a fight
Comes home happy
Wakes up sad
Says 'What the hell, it can't be bad.'
'To get *popped up*, and spend your dough.'
'Easy come, easy go.'

What is life, if you can't booze
Sup your pint lad,
You can't lose.
Lift your ale and down it quick.
Have another in half a tick.
Don't forget to get some cigs
Smoke and drink, t' back to the digs
Soon tomorrow night will come
. . . no cigs! I'll go and get me some.
While I'm out, I'll have a beer.
Wife understands,
She knows I'm here.

I need to drink - she knows the score
Oh! While I'm here, I'll have one more.
Wife sits waiting.
But in vain,
While Husband's saying;
'What's yours again?'

Nora Smith

WORKING BLUES

Do I need an action plan to set my life in store?
Do I need objectives to gain rewards galore?
Do I need to brainstorm the pros and cons of money?
Is the end result a land of milk and honey?

Can I not be satisfied with what I have right now?
Or is in life a career the very sacred cow?
One certainly gains a salary, pensionable for old age
But in the meantime one is trapped within the success cage

And when I'm sixty and I've strived for that golden ball
Will I have my health and drive, or will I suddenly fall
Shall I think of all those years given to the firm
Soldiering on regardless, thinking only of long term

Now here I am still young and bright, the future looking sunny
So why do I whittle and worry about the dreaded money
Perhaps because society directs us to achievement
And can forget to include in this happiness and contentment

Without a job of recognition
Should one feel low and small
Is in life the only mission
To work and get it all?

Diane Birtwisle

MIGHT AS WELL BE A FLY

Oh me oh my
Might as well be a fly
Trying to reach a cold apple pie
Waiting around all day
While the other arf
Drinks merrily away
Even a fly has more excitement
Than I
Oh me oh my

Just like a spider
The barmaid waits
She just bides her time
She knows he'll come by
In a little while
Always trying to drink
The pubs dry
Oh me oh my
I just give a big sigh

I feel as though I've
Been sprayed with DDT
Pity I'm not sprayed with whisky
On Saturday or Sunday
He sometimes stays in
Because he's tired.
And has to give in
No words we speak
He just lies down
And goes to sleep.

Janet Hannan

MAYBE

As I pace this empty street,
The light fades above.
What must I have done
To lose your love?

What must I have said
To drive you away?
What did she do
To make you stay
All night
And all day?

Raging, screaming,
Begging, pleading,
Crying, watching
You leaving me.

Wondering how many more times
Your eye will stray.
Maybe . . .
. . . It's better this way?

Margaret Nicol

THE SPRING

In the Spring the bluebells ring
The birds in the trees begin their mating
And all the moles come out of their holes to
see what's going on
In May when it is such a lovely day
The children love to play in the meadows
Grassy fields where they can smell the
sweet fresh hay.

Jean Jukes

STATE OF THE WORLD

Just look and see, what bad deeds,
The world has done, to those who need
Who need our love, and our care,
So why is life so unfair.

They twist their little minds so much,
That childhood is lost, so out of touch,
They keep the guilt hidden inside,
It hurts them so, it takes their pride,

There not the ones, that are to blame,
So give them love, not all this shame,
Help them now, while there young,
Tell them that they've done no wrong.

Their only children, you were too
Would you like it if it happened to you?

Karin Clarkson

AUTUMN MORNING

When I wake in the chill of the morning,
I see through my window pane
The colourful charm of Autumn
Which never for me will wane.

The grey morning mist slowly rising,
A curtain, rolled back, and behold -
The garden a riot of colour
Of crimson and purple and gold.

The hedges are heavy with berries
And sunlit, pearl spangled with dew;
While I catch on the distant horizon
A glimpse of a cornfield's rich hue.

Margaret Thomas

BODY AND SOUL REUNITED

Sometimes, the soul takes flight,
Travels alone, save for the eyes of the mind,
And leaves the body, gone out like a light.
Just an empty vessel is left behind.
It journeys on, until you are found,
And knows again the gentleness of your touch.
I long to scream, but cannot make a sound,
For such caresses have I yearned so much.
My body and soul are reunited in you,
Electric shocks of pleasure are coursing through my veins.
If you were gone, I know not what I'd do,
For the life you have emblazoned would never be the same.

Vanessa Rivington

CHRISTMAS EVE

I tiptoe cross the landing.
And creep on down the stair
Has he been and gone or is he still there?
Everything is silent just a distant bell rings
Everywhere is shining bright with tinsel and things.
Suddenly a movement, a shadow by the door
Goodness me that's him, it's got to be for sure,
Flying up the stairway I dare not make a sound
Fast asleep in my bed that's where I must be found.
I pull the covers round me and snuggle down so tight
To the sound of distant Carollers singing *Silent Night*
I drift into my childish sleep and dream my magic dreams
And out across the starlit sky to the winking moon he beams,
And as he travels homeward the snow begins to fall,
It's going to be a wonderful white christmas after all.

Evette Robinson

POTATO HARVESTING

The peace of the mellow morning
No noise upon the still ground
The sun sets no light upon mushrooms
Their wild state repose in the round.

It's the season when the potatoes
Can no longer reside in the ground
The horses still out in the dewy fields
They can hear familiar voices around

Can they, dare they ignore their beckoning
A heavy work day lieth ahead
When with collars and reins and heavy carts
Would your heart not lie like lead.

But their desires for chaff and hay
Much mixed with water and love
Overtake the thoughts of this work laden day
From low meadows they come up above

The silence of morning is broken
Here come the galloping hooves
The dewy mushrooms are scattered afar
Under the four footed rooves

The sound of the galloping hooves
Is replaced by snuffling and whinnies
Those velvet muzzles in mangers are shoved
Albeit not groomed for the guineas.

As on go collars and saddles
As clip clop go the hooves.
And the heavy carts break again the morn
Harvest farming is crops from the grooves.

J Faulkner

DON'T THEY KNOW

There are no jobs in the papers or on shop doors and boards,
Not through lack of trying are so many unemployed.
The news, is rife in telling us firms are closing down,
I know I'm not the only one who needs a few more pounds.

It's very clear there are no jobs with so many signing on,
We cannot all be classed as yobs when all the work has gone.
It seems so very strange to me the DSS don't know,
They haven't heard there is no work or don't they let it show.

The unemployment office treat me like a nerd,
We're individual people not a cattle herd.'
We surely know there is no work absurd they have not heard.
Each six months they summon us for an interview,
They ask us why we've found no work and realy make us stew.

At whatever age it seems you are, perhaps not so young nor over
                                                              hill,
Yet from the person sitting there those greeting looks could kill.
Do this do that are heard to say as if still twenty five.
It being very hard to comprehend are we meant to stay alive.

Obvious they don't know what it's like with good job and pay,
does it take so very much
                    treating us a nicer way?

Audrey P S Williams

71

WHERE ANGELS CALL HOME

Your heart was ripped out
Leaving a body without life
Your future is in shreds
Who struck cold with the knife?

They didn't mean to harm you
Or so they often say
Will they get a life sentence
Are they really going to pay?

Eventually we all die
But you were far too young
And we are all sat missing you
What have those murderers done?

They were finally found guilty
And sentenced to many years
But you still suffered all that pain
And we cried all those tears.

Time will be the hardest
And the time that they're set free
I know I want to kill them
For taking you from me.

But I know I couldn't do it
My heart just isn't that cold
So, I must put the pieces back
Of my broken, shattered world.

I know you can't be hurt now
And you'll never feel alone
No evil can touch you ever again
In a place, the angels call home.

Marie Ness

BE GRACEFUL

Come over here and let me see.
Stretch your neck and turn around,
Yes you look good to me,
Keep your hair hung straight down,
Eyes open wide now pout your lips,
Stand up straight with hands on hips.
Slowly turn and walk away.
Don't forget your rear to sway.
All your movements come together.
Step with the feet light as a feather.
Curtain up, the lights are bright
Yes sire the girls just right.

Barry Fletcher

SCHOOL DAYS

Just one more time
That is all I can take.
You call me names
Then beat me to death.
Time's on your side
As nothing is done,
I try to run wide
But! you have to have your fun.
Why was I born,
If this is my fate?
All of your words
Are all too late.
School is so cruel
As some of us don't learn,
Only to bully, boy or girl.
Teachers might try
But words are all lies.
As I lick my wounds
All alone in my room,
When I am dead
Will you speak kind words
To make you feel better,
To save your face, with grace.
Will all who are bullied
Have no more sunrise, rainbows?
Cowering in terror, each their ways
Surviving in memories of sorrows,
All of your school days.

M B Such

74

- OUR FIREPLACE -

It stood in the middle of the parlour wall,
With the mantelpiece 'twas nearly six feet tall;
Cast iron, black leaded 'til it shone,
You could see your face when you looked upon . . .
Our fireplace:

It had an oven where Mam baked bread and bap,
A tank for hot water, with a little brass tap;
In between, the fire, always burning bright,
It cheered us up and warmed us on many a chilly night . . .
Our fireplace:

The mantelpiece, at each end a china pug,
A clock in the centre, at each side a Toby jug;
A skirt of velvet, with little bobbins hanging down,
It was a most welcoming sight after shopping in the town . . .
Our fireplace:

Down below, the fender, emery papered 'til it gleamed,
The cat curled up and cosy softly purring as it dreamed;
Brass handled poker, brass handled rake,
Stood always at the ready to rejuvenate . . .
Our fireplace:

Roasting chestnuts, toasting bread on a long long fork,
Lots of childish laughter mixed up with family talk;
Every house in our street had a fireplace,
                        this comes as no surprise,
But if there'd been a competition . . . it would have won first prize . . .
Our fireplace:

Vernon L Hawks

THE LANE

I walked the lane again last night
That long and lonely lane,
Beneath the glow of lantern light
I searched for you in vain.
I marked each step along the way
The sky was clear above
The moon looked down in sympathy
As I waited for my love.
The minutes slowly ticked away
My hands and feet were numb.
As was my heart, my aching heart,
Yet still you didn't come.
Two lovers walked by hand in hand,
They didn't seem to care,
I'll walk the lane again tonight,
And maybe you'll be there.

Marjorie V Lewis

A CHERRIE LITTLE DITTIE

I am a quiet person.
I'm really very shy,
But when I have too much to drink,
My spirits just let fly.
They take me to the Milky Way,
Then fly me onto Mars.
I end up singing merrily
Sitting on the stars.

Mary Simmonds

PLEASING MYSELF

It's not all that bad, reaching sixty-five
It's like being reborn, and I'm glad I'm alive,

No more early mornings, and watching the clock,
My alarm now resides in the drawer, in a sock.

And instead of Monday being the day that I dread,
I roll over, and pull the quilt over my head.

On Tuesday, it's no more being nagged at by you,
I'll pack up a picnic, and go to the zoo.

Then Wednesday, I'm off to an *Old time dance*,
Not checking off orders fresh in from France.

And Thursday, I'm taking a leisurely stroll,
You'll find me relaxed at the nineteenth hole.

Then Friday, I'll pick up my *Crinkly Bus Pass,*
I can go where I want to, no questions asked.

And on the weekend, I'll be thinking of you,
You see dear old Boss, I feel sorry for you.

Under all that pressure at a mere twenty-two
I'll bet you'll be glad when you're sixty-five too.

See, your day will come for the big office do
You'll find that they give the same present to you

You too, will receive the *Great Gold Plated Clock,*

Just take it from me.

Stick it in a sock.

Lyn Round

CLICKETY CLICK

Back and forth, back and forth,
The shuttle of the Hartersley loom.
In the old rusty tin shed,
He's producing masterpieces.

The pattern emerging,
In view of the master's hand.
The pattern for the next life,
Passing out of human sight.

Here today, gone tomorrow.
The clock ticking away,
Getting closer to the threads of eternity.
A weaver, an elder, a chum,
Sadly missed.

Iain M MacLeod

TO THE RESCUE ON THE WESTERN LAWNS

The Police Force, Fire Brigade and Ambulance Crews
All worked together to release a driver trapped,
When they displayed their skills in rescues.
On this their demonstration Day.

The Coastguards who man lights on house and ship
To guide our ships from dangers they cannot see.
And our Lifeboatmen who rescue those in need
Whether on beach or high cliffs or at sea.

First Aid and further help was shown
By heart massage and mouth to mouth resuscitation
On a life like model tried and tried again.
Until the sign of joyful restoration.

The Firemen proudly showed their lofty ladder
And up and up and round and round it went.
While children queued for a nostalgic ride
On an engine red and long since retired.

So whether we be on ship or shore
We can always rest assured
That our rescue crews are always there
To answer nine nine nine whenever called.

Music was played by our Eastbourne duo so well.
The Silver Band in their scarlet blazers bright.
And the Scottish Pipes in their swirling kilts
Kept our feet tapping as they smartly marched by the right.

Kenneth James Brown

RINGS ON THEIR FINGERS

About two years ago Tina first came to tea
The right girl for Nick it was easy to see
We liked her immediately, and still feel the same
Even more than before now she has our surname.

She walked up the aisle on her proud father's arm
Looking beautiful in white, and wonderfully calm
Their parson, a friend of the parents and bride
Said that to marry them gave him pleasure and pride

High in the tower of King's Lynn *St Faith's* church
Bellringers peered down from their lofty perch
Prior to the service they had set the bells pealing
To enhance the occasion, and the wedding day feeling

One part of the ceremony, when rings were exchanged
Went rather less smoothly than had been arranged
On the bride's knuckle the gold band did linger
And had to be forced over her quite dainty finger.

As husband and wife they walked back down the aisle
Where the photographer waited and asked them to smile
Then off to the reception with family and friends
Wishing their big day to have the happiest of ends.

Helped by her husband the bride cut the cake
Which she and her mother had decided to make
I heard the groom say it was nice and tasty
But was he telling the truth, or playing for safety?

Sometime later the newlyweds slipped quietly away
Keen to start married life without further delay
They drove to the airport to catch a night plane
For an idyllic honeymoon in more sunny Spain.

F W Bowman

THE FOUR SEASONS

Waiting, waiting, anticipating
The wonderful joy of spring
The flowers that grow in the hedgerow
The songs the happy birds sing.

Longing, longing for when beaches are thronging
Everyone's down to the sea,
The mornings are hazy
The afternoon lazy
There's strawberries and cream for tea.

Sighing, sighing, everything's dying
The golden leaves fall to the ground.
Summer has gone, the birds have flown
Mother Nature is wearing a frown,

Dreading, dreading, when snow is spreading
The nights get longer and colder.
At the Winter's demise
We all realise
That we are another year older.

G Bullman

WALKIES

Missus was a Major
In an army nursing corps.
Susie was a dachsie
With a tummy on the floor.

Missus walked so upright
With a steady measured pace,
Susie had no option
But to keep there in her place -

Half a yard behind her Missus
When they went out for a walk,
Susie pattering bravely
As Missus on would stalk.

She couldn't always make it.
No matter how she tried,
Her lead would tighten - tighten,
Missus never broke her stride.

So Susie started flying.
Her short legs went berserk -
She scrabbled for a foothold
And landed with a jerk,

And gamely went on running.
Her tail was like a plume
Waving bravely in the slipstream,
Missus, I'll catch up soon.

Norma Benstead

CRY WITHIN A DREAM

I did not grieve like all the rest
Just a glazey stare that was my best
I did not mean to be like this
It was all to quick no reminisce
I loved my dad the pains within
I sometimes think I have done a sin.

Ten years had past and then one night
I had a dream so clear and bright
My mum and dad both crying together
Hands held out for comfort forever
I took their hands my eyes welled with tears
Which helped me out of those inner years
Let me take you home but my words were dying
I saw no more but I kept on crying
Why do I cry within a dream but did not grieve like all
the rest.

The dream so real I can't explain
I awoke to the feel of falling rain
The falling rain was a part of me
I was awake and crying at the memory
After all this time I don't know why I cried and grieved
Like all the rest.

K W Butler

PANORAMA PANORAMA

The Grandeur I see before me
Gives great pleasure to my eye
Like to my ear, did the orchestral suite
I heard first, as a small boy.

The hills seem so pleasingly near
And so too, the mountains, tipped with white
As over the wispy cloud they appear
In itself tis a beautiful sight.

The colour of the meadow
Sloping ever upward, a vivid green
Meeting the fir trees, swooping low
Through the seasons, showing the same sheen.

The grey of the rocky outcrop
As with the Spring colours it blends
With the first flower, the snowdrop
The slope moves, as the breeze, its gentle head bends.

As I gaze on this Panorama
My thoughts are as ever turned to you
There is no word of English grammar
That can describe you, and your beauty too.

Len Beddow

RHYME AND REASON

The litter blows along the street,
Hard grey pavement under your feet,
You don't care,
There remains no grass
The day of the animal come to pass
You don't care
The tele's on all day
Farmers burn all the hay.
You don't care
The hole in the ozone grows bigger each day.
Soon we shall have to pay
You don't care
Don't let the ice caps melt,
Clean up the world which once healthily smelt,
Show everyone you care.
Don't take water from the rivers
Grow some grass for the snake that slithers,
Show everyone you care.
Put the television away
Let the horses have the hay
Show everyone you care
Stop the ozone hole from growing,
Get out in the field and start sowing
Show everyone you care.
Use the buses - it's cleaner
Help the trees leaves to be greener,
Let's make tomorrow's day,
A cleaner, greener one, heh!

Jean Acott

ON YOUR WEDDING DAY

With age comes
　　　Knowledge,
With knowledge comes
　　　Love,
With love comes
　　　Friendship,
With friendship comes
　　　Marriage,
With marriage comes,
　　　Togetherness,
In everything you do.
May happiness be always
　　　With you both.

Pauline Clark

ASK YOURSELF

Are the living ungrateful, are the loving untrue.
Is the misery in the world suddenly affecting you?
Are you feeling miserable, sad, or ill at ease.
Sorry for yourself at times, difficult to please.
Do you argue with your friends
Or battle on your own.
Turn your back on something good,
When to you it has been shown.
Are you selfish, are you greedy,
Do you have a wicked streak.
Get everything that you desire.
From those a little weak
Have you said those few small words
To upset a pal that's dear,
Are you thinking evil things
Of someone who is near.
If thinking of these things alone
Just put them on the shelf.
You might be doing someone harm
Why not ask yourself?

D Rochester

THE COTSWOLDS

I lifted my eyes and thus did I see
Beauty - Serenity just meant for me
My thoughts could not share this wondrous place
Where life holds its hand. Life stops its pace
What can I say of all I behold
Evening of year had come to this Wold
Soon I must leave my new found peace
Return to where noise will not cease
When will I wander again in these hills
The Cotswolds country where loveliness spills
Lord in his heavens is generous to me
But he bequeaths all his handwork also to thee
Whilst in the City I pray and I hope
Through turmoil and dust and pungent car smoke
Here I lift up my eyes to the rich hills
And pray for the day . . . That's if God wills
I will walk with my peace in the green dales
Listen to birds singing their tales
I will have time to stand and stare
Grass under my feet . . . Mist in my hair
Follow the river along Shakespeare's Avon
And know myself for I've found my haven.

Grace Graham

THE HARDEST THING OF ALL

It's so hard
Watching your grandchildren at play
Knowing you'll never see their wedding day.
Watching the baby start to crawl,
Will he remember you at all?

It's so hard
Sitting gazing out to sea,
Holidays that will never be;
No more visiting old friends,
Just the postcards that they send.

It's so hard
Those retirement schemes you made,
All those happy plans you laid;
Looking forward to the day
Work would finish - then away!

But the hardest thing of all
Is to helplessly stand by
And watch your loved one die,
Knowing what he sees in his mind's eye.

Anne Horne

I SEE

I see the trees, so plush and green.
I see the hay fields, yellow and clean.

I see the river, rolling by.
I see the beautiful, blue sky.

I see the children, laughing and crying.
I see the adults, caring and smiling.

I see the world, coughing and choking.
I see the animals, dead and dying.

I see the flowers, wilting and sighing.
I see the human race, not really trying.

I see it all *dead* . . .

John Cameron

HOPES

I care so much in my heart
Please Lord give me that start
My life is for a purpose, of
reasons and hope, and time
to spread it out.

There's so many things I'd
like to do, perhaps write a book
or two.
Share my life with others
And look at photos old and new.

Walk to Gretner Green, and ride a
horse coming back.
Be a clown for a day
and meet a old lady very grey.

Meet someone important in my time
Perhaps the Queen it would be divine.
See a spaceship go to the moon
And perhaps that shouldn't be too soon.
Go up in a hot air balloon
And ride upon a horse and cart

So many things I'd like to do
But I wouldn't know how to start
All these things are from my heart
Please guide me there
For the start.

K R Frost

DOUBLE TROUBLE

My name is Geoffray Exeter
I am a common worm
My mummy's very pregnant
She's almost reached full term

I'll soon have lots of siblings
(To you, sisters and brothers)
She and I and us and them
Exactly like the others

The garden's wet, the grass is lush
We've really got it made
But, who's this coming down the path?
The gardener with his spade

My name's now Geoff, Ray's over there
With Chris, and Fred's with Tina
Eric's with Jon, Nathan's with Les
Where's Lee - has no-one seen her?

The spade has chopped us all in half
My mummy had a *Benny*
Until she counted up her bairns
And found she'd twice as many

We're going to have a party tonight
And forget this fiddle-faddle
I've seen this doll named Glenda so
Gimme my boots and *saddle.*

Lynn Morley

THE HAUNTED MILL

There's a spooky old mill at the top of graves hill.
Its shafts rigid and silent, the sails deathly still.

You hear not a murmur, a creek, or a sigh,
Consumed by a terror if you have to walk by.

No matter how gale force the raging winds blow,
That ominous wind mill refuses to go.

But I've heard the mill turns on one special night,
When travellers are drawn by its strange mournful sight.

They've heard all the rumours of fiction or fact,
Of those who go looking and never come back,

Yet, some are oblivious to fears of this kind,
And carry straight on, ignoring the sign!

Beware of this mill! In large letters it read!
To instill in the curious unthinkable dread

But, on up the steps, and in through the door,
Now the shafts start a stirring, the sails turn once more,

Then, above all the creaking and groans from that mill,
There's a loud piercing scream, then all becomes still.

Yes! not even a trace of a hair, flesh, or thread.
Although, it's for certain, the foolhardy are dead.

But listen all you doubters if skeptic your prone,
Come! I'll show you their blood! stained, on the millstone!

Carol Fay Clarke

UNTITLED

I have butterflies in my tum
And my palms begin to sweat
The trembling has begun
Although it's not time yet.
'Your symptoms I've known,' my best friend said.
'You know - cotton wool for brains,
And feet just like lead.'
I have a tense headache
As I bravely wave goodbye.
Then, horror of horrors
I begin to cry.
Oh what a specimen - what a poor tool!
The reason?
It's my daughters first day at school.

J Hudspeth

THE HOUSEWIFE AND THE SALESMAN

It was one Monday evening just after nine
I answered the door as I heard the bell chime
A young man stood there with a flashing smile
He said I'd like to come in and talk for a while
Like a fool I took him into my home
But I wouldn't now, if I had only known.

He dashed to his car and brought in a large Hoover
It's great for dirt and a stain remover
He opened a bag and threw dust on the floor
I'd only swept it the day before.
'My,' he said, 'this carpet is full of dirt.'
I gave a sniff, I was really quite hurt.
I pride myself in keeping it clean.
'Don't worry,' he said 'it's not the worst I have seen.'

He said, 'Let's go upstairs, see what we can find.'
Like a lamb to the slaughter I trailed behind.
'Do you know,' he said, 'your mattress is full of mites
Haven't you noticed, do you get any bites?'
'And under the bed there's a heap of fluff
But, watch, this will soon get rid of the stuff
It's full of germs and every day they renew
It's a wonder you look as well as you do.'

I staggered downstairs, my head in a daze
And on he went to the second phase
At last, I said, 'how much do we pay?'
He changed the subject he just wouldn't say.

After two coffees and a cup of tea
Still he kept on talking endlessly
Two hours later at eleven, maybe a quarter past
My husband remarked, are you planning to stay for breakfast.

D Jeffery

WHY?

Why are the clouds
round, white and fluffy
Why on a fox cub
is it always stuffy
Why are flowers
so wild and rare
How do lice climb
in your hair
Why do chickens
meet their fate
Every Sunday on my plate
     Oh why
     Oh why
     Oh why.

Emma Jones

TELLY ADDICTS

Geroff yer bum an' goo art ter play
Yer shudn't sit 'ere in doors all day;
Yer'll ev square eyeballs afore yer ten:
Gerrup an' gerrart - Ah won't tell yer agen!

When Ah wurra lad we ed no TV
But we found lots to do me brother an' me.
Me Dad wernt well-off - e didn't ev ote
So we med ar own fun wi little or note.

Footer we played in a gang on the rec,
Then arter dinner ar five-stones wid tek
An' sit in the backyard throwing ar snobs
Gooin' through *scrambles cracks* and *fly dobs*.

Agen the yard wall ar fagcards wid skim
Me brother an' me, an' allus Ah beat 'im.
If we ed a few pence to spend at the shop
Wid buy arsens *marlies* or praps whip an' top.

Gerrup an' gerrart - dincha 'ear worra sed?
Doon't sit theer grizzlin' an' scratchin yerred
Gerrup an' gerrart an' goo art ter play
- Cos Ah'm gooin' ter watch nar -
                    It's *Match o' the Day!*

Charles Robinson

TORQUAY

High on a hill stood our hotel when we stayed in Torquay,
And from the lovely dining room we could see the distant sea.
To reach the town down down we went, down winding paths and
then
We climbed down over one hundred steps and crossed a stretch of
green.

At last we reached the harbour where we sniffed the salt sea breeze.
The seagulls shrieked, the fountains played among the fine palm
trees.
Liam ran on the rust red sand, the sea tried to reach his shoes
But he jumped away as the waves crept in trying to wet his toes.

We found treasure, sparkling shiny shells, in the rust red sand.
We jumped over little pebbly pools on the weed strewn strand.
We made footprints on firm damp sand, treading where none had
gone before,
Until all too soon it was time to leave that rust red sandy shore.

Sifting soft sand from our salt stained shoes we left the rust red bay;
The salt wind blew and in the sunshine shone rainbow drops
of spray.
As we walked back towards the town we saw many boats large and
small,
Some of which were nestling snugly, berthed beneath the harbour
wall.

At noon we sat on a bench to eat, near some lovely flowerbeds.
Out of the sky swooped the pigeons, to sit on our arms and heads.
We decided to move away, as they were making such a fuss,
And we laughed, as looking back we saw them, waddling after us.

Later beneath a towering cliff we found a different beach,
No rust red sand here, just pebbles and stones, as far as the eye
could reach.
The waves rushed in rattling the pebbles, with a wet and watery
crash.
We flung stones into the sea, where they fell with a satisfying splash.

Liam was King of the Castle on that deserted pebbly shore.
We heard the windblown cry of the gulls, and the sound of the sea,
nothing more.
The sun sank slowly in the west, gleaming gold on the restless swell.
We left our enchanted kingdom before the shadows of twilight fell.

April Barry

THE TELESCOPE

Then, I pressed the telescope to mine eye;
And lo! I saw this vision from afar;
A lost world spun 'neath darkening sky,
Illuminated by a dying star.
A world that never saw the face of man;
Down light years lost since time began.
There was no day - nor ever came a night;
Setting alien stars alight,
To marvel at its weird angled moon -
'Twas twilight only in the hoarie noon;
Whilst hurricanes of monstrous force,
Across its barren surface course;
Driven, howling forever more,
Along a lonely sea-less shore.

I took the eyepiece from mine eye,
And, ah! it was so sweet -
To see again our friendly Earth;
The traffic rolling down our street.

Edward M Shipsey

BECKONING OF THE SEASONS

The scent of bluebells
In a shady wood.
The glistening sheen of celandines
In the hedgerow stood.
With the golden glow of colts foots
On a grassy hill
Followed by dandelions and wild daffodil.
All enjoyed in my youthful days
And continue on in so many ways.

F G Challenger

SUMMER RIDE

As I ride along a motorway
On a bright summer day
I observe the glorious scenes
As we pass along the way.
The abundant green trees
On the hills and dales
The lovely blue sky as it
Joins with the dales.
Oh what pleasure it gives
As we travel on the way
To behold such glory
On a busy highway.
It truly remains with me
For many a day
I am eternally grateful
For such a day.

June Misson

HAPPY SUNSHINE HOURS

In the valley where the trees
dance a ballet with the breeze,
and the roses nod sweet heads in approval.
Wafting perfume all about,
while the children laugh and shout,
and the bees are working hard,
collecting nectar, while the bard,
sits idly watching,
drinking in these sights with wonder.
Butterflies are too and fro,
and the earth is all aglow,
with its fruits and its flowers,
full of happy sunshine hours.
Making all the winters toil,
seem worthwhile, ah, happy hours.

P E Langton

MILLIONAIRE

If I were a millionaire my friend
I wouldn't mop this floor
Or clean the brass
Or dust the chair
Or any other chore.

I'd find an army of seven or eight
To keep this homestead clean and straight
They'd mop and polish and dust and scurry.
To please this mistress they'd have to hurry.

Then I'd sit back and ponder the sight
While the oven like magic is cleaned
Oh so bright.
Then I could garden or laze in the sun
To be a millionaire oh what fun.

Sylvia Salisbury

THE LOSS OF A CHILD

Your stay on earth is ended,
Your little soul's set free,
It was as God intended,
Though it's hard for us to see.

In heavens garden up above,
You'll laugh and sing and play.
And God will give you tender love,
And keep you safe each day.

Hilary Peck

HIGGER TOR

The blackened heather stiffly lies,
Beneath the cloudless blue spring skies.
It's carpet threaded here and there,
With light green paths of wear and tear.

Some stony steps lead to the top,
To closely view old Higger's crop.
The sun reveals a hint of steel,
As youngsters much prefer two wheels.

The mountain bike makes life astride
A simple task, and easy ride.
While hiking folk take time to stare,
The bikers race, to reach somewhere.

I'll sit awhile, and take it in,
No more desire to climb or spin.
Just write a poem in Higger's praise,
I'm satisfied with lazy days.

Dilys Paulson

UNTITLED

What is a mother?
What can I say?
Who else works 24 hours a day.

Who is there in the morning
To get you out of bed
Calling up the stairs
Wake up you sleepy head.

Who puts her arms around you
When things are getting tough
Who always seems to know
Just when you've had enough.

Of this crazy mixed up world
Where things get you down
Where friends who used to smile
Now give you a frown.

Ah yes once again, it's dear old mother
Who's ever close at hand
Helping you to bear
The things you cannot understand.

So if you have a mother,
Take her by the hand
Tell there's no-one like her
Living in this land.

For as sure as God's in heaven
She'll stick by you through thick and thin
Your mother a gift from God
So give all your thanks to him.

Hilda Coe

THE RIVER WALK

As I walk along the river bank,
I see a kingfisher sitting on a plank
eyeing up its minnowie prey.
Then there's a dart - what a display!
To see a kingfisher in full flight,
no word to explain it - what a sight!
I walk a little further along,
and there's a thrush singing out its song.
There's a fisherman in water deep
trying to catch a trout - you must creep.
I look around and see a sight -
reflections in the water bright.
The sun overhead its redden glow,
what a sight to behold, you know.
Oh! I do like my river walk,
it's peaceful and quiet - you don't have to talk.
I walk over to the edge
and peep through the weed and clover bed.
To my surprise there's a trout fast asleep
in waters not too deep.
I must not knock a pebble in
to make a ripple or she will swim.
I do love my river walk,
peace and quiet - and no talk.
Further down the river bank I see a heron.
Shush, I must stalk
or I will frighten it.
Creep, don't walk.
As I walk away whistling out a song,
I've been lucky today to creep and walk
Along.
There's only one person to thank for all this -
That's the Lord God - what heavenly bliss!

Terrence McIntyre

SPRINGTIME

I feel that spring is in the air,
Flowers protruding everywhere
The tulips stand all array,
Oh what a beautiful springtime day.
The daffodils stand so proud
A hint of dew on their golden shroud
The birds are singing way up high.
The sun is gleaming in the sky
People whistling saying 'How do you do?'
Is spring really here can it be true,
Baby lambs skipping around bleating as they go.
Spiders webs gently blowing to and fro.
Springtime is one of those splendid things,
All the beauty and colour mother nature brings.
We all must appreciate for this reason
The joy and happiness of this season.

F M Joynes

CHRISTMAS CHEER

Christmas comes but once a year, and Santa's on his way,
With all the toys, for girls and boys, and a turkey for Christmas day,
The shops are lit with fairy lights, the lamps are all aglow,
The pavements full of shoppers, making footprints in the snow.

With all the hustle, and the bustle, things are so exciting,
There's presents to buy, cards to post, and they all need writing,
Plum pudding's made, the fires ablaze, mince pies decked with holly,
The Christmas cake looks very good, a time for making jolly.

With paper hats, and crackers, the parties will be swinging,
Blind mans buff is so much fun, and the children will be singing,
Songs of Christmas, and the wise men, in days of long ago,
About the holly and the ivy, and good old mistletoe.

It's Christmas eve, the church is lit with candles on a tree,
The organ is playing carols, and there's a crib to see.
All for our dear Lord Jesus, who was born in a stable bare,
He came down to save us, and surround us with his care.

Doris West

SPECTACLES . . .

Spectacles are worn by lots of folks,
Some people think they are a big joke.
We really need them for our sight,
They give us endless times of delight.
There are some times they get up our nose,
We could remedy this I suppose.

Rain is one of the biggest culprits,
Steamed up glasses cause us to trip.
I wish I'd got windscreen wipers we've always said,
That's it the problems solved, as ideas rush through my head.
An invention is called for so it seems,
Now to think of ways and means.

A microchip fitted in glasses arms,
Just behind our ears will do us no harm.
Fine wire running through them no-one can see,
Will still enhance and fit us to a tee.
Tiny wipers made especially for lenses,
Hooked to our microchip sensors.

How to switch on this wonderful invention,
Needs lots of thought and careful attention.
Remote control buttons a cough or a sneeze,
We need something that's easy just a breeze.
A sensor in the nose bridge is a notion,
Needing two taps to put in motion.

Now to try them in the rain,
Lets hope they won't be too much of a pain.
Oh what joy my creations bliss,
To cross the road isn't hit and miss.
They work as well when I'm all steamed up,
Now I get pleasure from not tripping up . . .

Jean Osborne

DARK THOUGHTS

We would sit at the end of dark entries on autumn and winter nights
Telling stories of ghosts and ghoulies and things that gave
                                        you a fright
Of the ghostly apparition living behind cellar doors
All afraid to collect the coal from beneath the wooden floors
Our toilets were outside across an unlit yard
No wonder we were good at school at running one hundred yards
You would sit on the loo bent over so your arm could reach the door
A creak outside would very near make you fall down on the floor
You would half sit there and shiver fearing the worst to arrive
As the noises still continued beyond the door outside
Eventually you decide you have to move to do the one hundred
                                        yard dash
And such relief as you reached the door of the kitchen in a flash
The old back door would slam loudly shut leaving you fully aware
That the darkness outside had been touching you as if a person
                                        was there.

Connie Barker

AN OLD MAN'S MEMORIES

The old man leaned upon the gate, and gave a tired sigh.
His mind was full of memories, of all his days gone by.
Alone, so alone, his family gone, no-one to share decisions,
An old man with his dreaming, not a young man with his visions.

His tired eyes wandered round the street, at people passing by,
Busy in their own small worlds, their hours flying high.
The housewife with her basket, and a baby in a pram,
The paper boy, the postman, the worker's traffic jam.

Amid the noise and bustle came the kids let out of school.
Laughing, shouting, happy now, no longer under rule.
He watched them all, he had the time, he'd nothing else to do,
Then memories flooded back to him, when he was like them too.

The games he'd played, the fun he'd had, the happy times of life,
And all the blessings he'd possessed, that far outweighed the strife.
The net for tiddlers in the brook, the bike that gave such pleasure,
The nuts he's gathered in the fields, the conkers he would treasure.

The day of pride in his first job, the weekend with his mates,
The Sunday suit, with shirt so white, to dress up for his dates.
His first, his last, his only love, the one he'd made his wife,
Who'd shared his sorrows and his joys. He'd had a happy life.

And as these memories filled his mind, the clouds that hovered o'er
And brought on all his loneliness, moved on, and were no more.
He left the gate, and wandered in. He smiled, and gave a nod.
And on his knees that night he said, 'I'm happy now, Dear God.'

Sylvia Needham

MOMENTS IN TIME

The choppy sea, the wind blowing offshore
Large breakers spewing their chested spore.
The land around corroded through history,
The tales that are told shrouded in mystery.
Awash at its base a strong current swirling stealthily by.
The gulls an odd puffin making known their presence,
The fauna and flora grimly clinging the vertical stance.
The odd rumble of a descending wave.
Crashing down to an empty cave.
Used by smugglers in days of yesteryear,
Piracy being the mariners worst fear,
An outcrop of menacing scraggy rock,
Where many a ship has run amock.
The natural sand bar awash with white foam,
A naive crew should never roam.
Big pebbles, some small dress a golden sand beach,
Strewn with deck chairs the tides cannot reach.
A hot lazy day the sun beating down,
The swimmers, the youngsters, sunbathers brown.
The yawls on the estuary a thriving sport,
Tacking away starboard then to port,
The hum of activity the uncanny drone,
The peace, the tranquillity, this is my home.

James Strawbridge

CHOBIE DAINTY

Hello! I'm Chobie Dainty.
A name unique to me.
I've been all over Europe,
Since nineteen-twenty-three.

Hello! I'm Chobie Dainty.
I came with lovely fair hair,
Pampered as a baby,
With tender loving care!

Hello! I'm Chobie Dainty.
Like others I went to Eton.
It was a strict old place,
Yet I was never beaten!

Hello! I'm Chobie Dainty.
And when the war was won.
I had a bad leg and one eye,
Believe me - that's no fun!

Hello! I'm Chobie Dainty.
Down to Oxford as a blue.
Really enjoyed my time there,
And left in fifty-two!

Hello! I'm Chobie Dainty.
And as the years roll by,
I'm a little scruffy now
And still only got one eye!

Hello! I'm Chobie Dainty.
Somewhat the worse for wear.
Not too bad really,
For a little teddy bear!

Lawson Phillips

TIME

Turn around, turn around,
Passions grow cold,
Babies are young men,
And young men are old.

Dreams of the future
Are all put away,
Time has gone past you,
It just couldn't stay.

Turn around, turn around,
Keep up the pace,
A year has gone past,
For the whole human race.

Summer has gone,
And the swallows have flown,
Leaves of October,
Have fallen and blown.

Turn around, turn around,
Hands of the clock,
Turn around, turn around,
Tick tock, tick tock.

W T Longman

PRAIRIE FARM

Once there were hedges on this plain
Where thrush and chaffinch made their nests,
Sheltered from stormy wind and rain,
Their singing made the spring time sweet.

Now all is silent, still and bare,
And gazing in the distance we
No longer glimpse the bounding hare
Take cover as he goes to ground.

For every species in a hedge
A hundred years increased its age
It sometimes marked a boundary edge
Dividing country parishes.

Maple, blackthorn, hazel, beech,
Hawthorn, elderberry, ash,
One hundred years established each
A unique feature of our land.

So many creatures sheltered there,
Shrew, vole and rabbit, e'en a fox
Would cunningly conceal his lair.
Now this small world has disappeared.

The blackthorn blossom hung like snow,
Later the hawthorn and wild rose
Scented the air and made a show
Of matchless beauty to catch the breath.

Creating this by Nature's way
Took centuries of patient growth.
Man has destroyed it in a day
And left a desert in its stead.

Kay Gilbert

THE BIGGEST GIFT

We had the biggest ever Christmas tree, the tallest in our street
With lights and chocolate Santa's, for us five kids to eat
There was tinsel all around it, and on the top a fairy
And close by stood a manger with Jesus, Joseph and Mary.

A great big open fireplace, with a great big roaring fire,
And bowls of nuts, and bowls of fruit, and all that you desire
And brand new bikes and brand new prams, and games and
toys galore
With talking dolls and walking dogs, who could have asked for more.

And wouldn't that be wonderful, if all of it were true,
But anything that we got was very rarely new.
There were no brand new bikes, nor prams, nor dolls, nor dogs,
nor toys,
There were no bowls of fruit or nuts, or other Christmas joys.

There was no roaring fire sat in our tiny grate
Just a tiny little flicker burning from an orange crate.
There never was a Christmas tree, with chocolates on to eat
You see we were that family, the poorest in our street.

Our mam worked every hour God sent through winter, spring
and summer
She had to work both day and night since our dad did a runner,
He preferred another woman, one who understood him see,
So now it's her and her kids that sit upon his knee.

But our Christmases were special, though our presents
they were few
It didn't really matter if they weren't always new.
Mum taught us to be grateful for what little bit we had
And being without possessions in no reason to be sad.

So looking back I wonder, just cos other kids got more
If we weren't that much better off because we were so poor
See we had a bigger, better gift, no reason to be sad.
The true love of a mother who gave everything she had.

J B A Roe

THE LITTLE OLD LADY

A little old lady with silver white hair
sits rocking away in her old rocking chair.
Her eyes bright with tears as her gaze comes to fall
on a handful of treasures stacked close to the wall.

That silly rag doll now so tattered and torn
a present from daddy, the day she was born.
And wrapped in a tissue with infinite care
are two dainty mittens that mum used to wear.

A smile finds its way to that age wrinkled face
as her gaze comes to rest on an old battered case.
For under the lid turning musty and brown,
her love letters wrapped in her silk wedding gown.

So few her possessions, yet each holds a key
to unlock secret doors in her long memory.
The chair that she rocks in, as day passes day
she once rocked her babies in just the same way.

A knock at the door, so she straightens her hair
and hoists herself out of her old rocking chair.
'I'll just get my bag, then I'm ready to go,
be careful, my suitcase, it's heavy you know.'

Now stepping outside through a dim wall of tears
she whispers goodbye to her happiest years.
The rest of her lifetime her footsteps will roam,
through gardens of flowers in an old peoples home.

Valerie Browning

PRINCE

A fluffy bundle of liver and white
How I remember he cried that night
And for many a night after that.
He chew the paper, shoes and mat.

There was no peace till he went to bed,
Against my wishes, let it be said.
It was with David he chose to sleep,
At the foot of the bed in a heap.

He's full of life, we can't tire him out,
Taking him walks all around about.
We took him in turns, but all in vain,
He just wagged his tail, and was ready again.

We lost him once for a complete day
He saw a rabbit, ran and lost his way,
We searched for him till it went dark,
Once we thought we heard his bark.

It was next morning he was found,
Many feet down a hole in the ground,
Prince was badly hurt, his leg was a mess
The vets good work, saved him I guess.

He plodded round with his back leg in plaster,
To many a dog, this would be a disaster.
But Prince persevered, his leg got strong
Now you wouldn't know, there had been anything wrong.

Now he's six and loved by all,
His behaviour when young we often recall,
But must admit, he's the family pet
By far the best we've ever met.

Shirley Travis

INFORMATION

We hope you have enjoyed reading this book - and that you will continue to enjoy it in the coming years.

If you like reading and writing poetry drop us a line, or give us a call, and we'll send you a free information pack.

Write to

Anchor Books Information
1-2 Wainman Road
Woodston
Peterborough
PE2 7BU.